Faith in Su

Jane Gibbs

Adult Educator

GROVE BOOKS LIMITED
RIDLEY HALL RD CAMBRIDGE CB3 9HU

Contents

To my father, who taught me the importance of fun.

The Cover Illustration is by Peter Ashton

First Impression September 2003
ISSN 0144-171X
ISBN 1 85174 540 8

Introduction: Something is Wrong in Suburbia

We lived in a pebble-dashed semi in the Home Counties which could have been almost any suburb in England. We were surrounded by houses and people, but you had to walk for half a mile before you could buy a newspaper—surrounded by life, yet never escaping the feeling that life was happening somewhere else. That's the suburbs.[1]

In the same week two committed evangelical clergy serving suburban parishes commented to us: 'I'm just not sure what I'm doing here any more.' For good or ill, an estimated 50–60% of the British population embraces the suburban way of life.[2] The suburban churches are the very ones to which the national church has until recently pointed as evidence of life. These churches, at least, could afford to pay their way. Whatever happened in the inner-cities, suburban churches could always be relied on to thrive. Not any more.

- Members of suburban congregations—however committed—simply cannot be relied on any more to attend worship every Sunday.[3]
- Competent and committed suburban lay people are more and more loth to take on regular church 'duties.' Everything has to be done on a rota basis. Suburbanites just do not seem to have the time for church activities any more.
- New Christians from our suburban church's Alpha course rarely make it as regular Sunday worshippers in church. In desperation, we are contemplating setting up a whole new service simply to stop them leaking away.

Something is wrong in suburbia.

As an attempt to unpack that 'something wrong,' this booklet makes uncomfortable reading. It is drawn from nearly 30 years of experience, first in a lay capacity and then as clergy-wife, divided roughly equally between a variety of inner-city and suburban parishes. The first two chapters examine the inherent characteristics of 21st-century suburbia and their impact on the church—if we are not careful. The last chapter suggests one change of approach which might help. Each chapter is followed by questions which might be used by individual readers or in small-group discussion.

2 Suburbia and its Culture

> In Britain's imagination the suburbs stand for dull, repetitive, default-mechanism lives, petty fake-Tudor or cod-Victorian brick and pebble-dash snobberies, for quiet desperation in the garage, furtive adultery in the conservatory, grimacing hypocrisy amid the Terry-and-June soft furnishings and a world view bought weekly from Waitrose.[4]

It is popular to be contemptuous of suburbia. Yet 'in Western Society… suburban residence appears to symbolize all the values of "good" living.'[5]

The origins of suburbia were filled with hope and ambition, from the nineteenth century 'railway suburbs' through to the classic suburban semis of the thirties. Then in the period immediately after World War Two the need for new housing acted as a catalyst. For the first time, people who perceived themselves as ordinary could both own their own homes and choose to live outside the cities where most of them worked. Suburbia embodied 'the attempt to marry town and country, and to create for middle classes, middle cultures in middle spaces in middle Britain.'[6] So the suburbs came to represent *liberation*—from poverty, pollution and proximity to neighbours. They also represented *choice*, set against which the inconvenience of travelling to work was considered relatively small.

Work-patterns in the 21st century have changed. Many people work from home or multiple work-bases.[7] As a result suburbia has spread wider and is no longer necessarily dependent on nearby cities for its survival. 'Suburbia' nowadays covers many different types of geographical area. It has been suggested that suburbia can be defined as the whole country minus cities and countryside, but even that ignores those places where suburbia has started to colonize the countryside.

A recent report for the Joseph Rowntree Foundation examining the sustainability of suburbs found a 'disturbing' lack of analysis of suburban areas.[8] In this context it has become popular to regard suburbia as a construct, a mindset, rather than a place. Suburbia epitomizes 'Middle England,' a way of living, a set of values which are widely accepted and have no need to be spelt out. But the JRF report lists no fewer than six different *geographical* types of suburb, concluding that the most significant are the two 'within which most suburban developments fit' in the UK. These are:

Public transport suburb	Medium density homogenous speculative suburbs, medium home-ownership, housing and services usually located near each other.
Car suburb	Low density homogeneous detached housing, high home ownership, often in an 'open' townscape fringe area (motorways, out of town shopping centres and golf clubs), pattern of housing, services usually dispersed.

Insofar, then, as it is still possible to identify Britain's suburbs in a geographical framework, those are the two definitions which will undergird the following pages.

Statistics relating to Gosforth, a suburban district of Tyneside, provide a good starting point for understanding what constitutes suburbia.[9] They give an interesting comparison of this area's demography with the UK average:

- *Age profile:* There are more elderly people, fewer children
- *Employment:* Unemployment is lower. 34% of households have more than one adult working. Over half the working population is employed in management, professional or technical occupations. There are more working women, especially self-employed ones.
- *Housing:* There are more rooms per household, more detached/ semi-detached homes and purpose-built flats. Owner-occupation is much more common, social housing much less so.
- *Education:* 30% of adults are educated to HND or higher.
- *Transport:* 64% go to work by car, rather than by bus or on foot. Multiple car ownership is almost double the Tyneside average. Fewer households have no car than in the wider population.

These few clues provide some evidence for the assertion that suburban living involves a whole mind-set, rather than simply a geographical location. *Choice* is still a fundamental part—choice of the right house, the right neighbours, the right schools and the right environment.

Individuals' definitions of 'right' in each context might, of course, differ. In practice, though, these choices underpin the very popularity of suburbia. They also help to bring about the homogeneity of many suburban areas— we choose to live alongside 'people like us.' The indications are that 'residential association is now built almost exclusively around similarity in economic rank.'[10] In extreme cases this can produce 'nimbyism'—a ghetto mentality simmering under the surface. In 1987 Robert Fishman went so far as to describe the classic suburb as 'a testimony to bourgeois anxieties, to deeply buried fears that translate into contempt and hatred for the "others" who inhabit the city.'[11] Even if that seems a little extreme, it does highlight a real issue: in my own comfortable piece of suburbia, many objections to a proposed new housing estate have revolved around the smaller new housing's not being 'in keeping' with the area.

Anyone hoping to minister in suburbia needs to invest some time in a social analysis of what confronts him or her. It is my observation that suburban culture tends towards certain clearly identifiable characteristics, and it is these which form the remainder of this chapter.

Desire for Space and Privacy

One of the central allures of suburbia has been the availability of *space*. The 'Tomorrow' report talks of 'a growing demand for larger homes, more easily built in the suburbs or beyond, driven by couples who aspire to middle-class lifestyles and identify this with suburban living.'[12] Liberation lies in having ones own boundaries marked out—hence the suburban obsession with fences, hedges and marker posts to delineate the amount of land owned by each resident household. There is an almost tangible wariness about allowing any but a carefully chosen few to cross the boundaries. The trouble with privacy, as Walter pointed out, is that 'no sooner have you achieved it than you have to start defending it.'[13] This contrasts starkly with our inner-city experience, where a neighbour three gardens away once came round spontaneously to help, having seen us struggling with repairs to our shed.

In suburbia it is not unusual to find carefully printed notices on front doors warning those without appointments not to call. Experience suggests that this is less to do with fear of crime than fear of being caught letting slip the often newly-adopted middle-class modus vivendi. If 'Humankind cannot bear very much reality,'[14] then suburban humankind seems able to bear even less. In the achievement-driven environment of suburbia, pain, difficulty and feelings of inadequacy are unacceptable. Whether perceived or real, the huge pressure to achieve 'success' amongst one's peers can lead to what Mark Stibbe calls 'a highly advanced technology of escapism'[15] where everyone covers their true personhood with a mask. Social intercourse outside work is often reduced to more or less formal dinner-parties booked weeks ahead. Although this may be seen as a function of the busyness of all the parties involved, it is also a very safe way of avoiding real conversation. 'Suburbia appears calm because stability is an essential longing. The need to create the appearance, to hang onto the dream, is a fundamental suburban need.'[16]

Autonomy and Control

If you or your parents have worked hard to acquire the resources needed to leave the grime of the city, it is not difficult to see how you might gladly espouse the philosophy that 'You get what you earn.' Your future success or failure, you believe, is under your own control. Being in control matters enormously. It is precisely this feature of life which is absent in much of the inner city, and therefore makes suburbia so different—'the ideal of a private environment over which one has total control.'[17] In suburbia 'I'm in charge. No-one tells me what to do or what to believe.' As Andre Godin has observed, 'those whose economic security is sufficient tend to develop a view of the world which centres on mastery through action.'[18]

In this climate choice is sacrosanct. During the many years we have spent living in Urban Priority Areas (UPAs), we have been poignantly aware that what marked us out from our neighbours—quite apart from anything tangible—was that we had the *choice* of moving away while they did not. Suburban consumers expect to choose in every department of life: a comfortable lifestyle; the best school for their children; the car or cars most suited to their lifestyle; the leisure activities and holidays which afford them the most appropriate relaxation. It is what Moynagh and Worsley call the 'it must fit me exactly mentality.'[19] The suburban philosophy expects goods, services and personal performance to be perfectly suited as of right.

Achievement

For many suburbanites achievement is paramount. Gibson Winter's observation in 1961 America still stands: 'The keynotes of [the style of the middle class] are activism and emphasis on achievements in gaining self-esteem.'[20] A frenzied activism is the hallmark of day-to-day life. All the available adults in a household will routinely be doing paid work, often stretching their working hours to the limits of domestic endurance. Holidays often suffer the overspill. A recent Times newspaper article quoted a recent study which found that 40% of employees now take their work with them on holiday.[21]

This dedication to paid work has a profound effect on all the generations. Grandparents—the young retired—are now frequently drafted in for childcare. So the leisure time they once had is eaten away. As for the children themselves, they inherit the drivenness of their parents. For years suburban parents have been prepared to move house in order to live in the catchment area of a 'good' school. Nor does it stop at the push for *academic* achievement. Out-of-school hours are spent acquiring extra skills—musical instruments, horse-riding, languages—or in extra tuition to boost school exam grades. Trying to organize a regular slot in our own parish recently for a confirmation class of three 13-year-olds almost foundered when the youth Filofaxes clashed. Suburbanites of all ages are marked by time-poverty.

Consumerism and Status

Achievement (in the suburban sense) brings an increase in disposable income, whose benefits start with the acquisition of goods. 'There is an intimate and indissoluble link between suburbia and buying.'[22] The £500bn spent annually by the people of Britain approximates to double the inflation-adjusted figure of 30 years ago. The degree of domestic comfort enjoyed today by many suburbanites would have been beyond the wildest dreams of their parents. 'Successful' suburbanites expect to accumulate capital.

Two implications of this trend are particularly relevant here. First, this 'commodified selfhood' causes people to assess their own worth in terms of their material goods. The original suburbs have been dubbed 'sites whose principal raison d'etre was the establishment of a person's individual identity.'[23] Nothing has changed. 'Consumer lifestyles provide a source of identity ...Life acquires meaning as we spend in ways that will impress our friends.'[24] (Our local branch of John Lewis had a spate of suburban customer complaints when it started to use delivery vans *without* the John Lewis logo.) In suburbia 'we've arrived and we want to demonstrate it.'

This mentality can have very damaging consequences, the most obvious of which is the debt spiral in which individuals and families are increasingly becoming trapped. It has more sinister results too.

> Because of the collapse of traditional relational networks and the way that material success has become a culturally-approved sign of worthwhile achievement, people right across all social classes are struggling to establish themselves as individuals of true worth, and the extent of the personal alienation that then ensues is leading to pathological behaviour patterns.[25]

Mobility

If paid work is your raison d-etre, then an employer's offer of promotion linked to a change of workbase cannot be ignored. Richard Keyes observes that 'Many adults now move every 3-5 years, whenever an old or new employer demands it. They uproot themselves and their families...in answering the call of upward mobility.'[26] As Philip Richter observes, there is an inherent paradox in suburban life: while its residents react strongly against change of any kind, one of the crucial forces which motivates them is dissatisfaction.[27] He calls it 'the dynamic of a sprinter who is unstable unless moving, and moves to keep balance.' There may well be second thoughts in families where there are secondary-aged children, but this tends simply to exacerbate the problem with younger employees, anxious to scale the promotion ladder as quickly as possible before being tied to one workbase for a while.

Of course, this has a serious knock-on effect on friendships. 'Length of residence is an important factor in increasing the circle of acquaintanceship, if not the intensity of relationship.'[28] While longer-term residents build neighbourly relationships over a period of time, those who are just passing through for a couple of years (which tends to equate to those with no secondary-age children) might regard it as a pointless exercise. As time passes, the relationships which count for a household become those which have stood the test of time and geography. Because they are usually at a distance, maintaining these friendships takes valuable leisure time, especially at weekends.

Social Intercourse

So mobility brings with it another unavoidable characteristic of suburbia. 'In general, the intercourse which creates a social fabric of neighbourhood is almost obliterated by residential mobility.'[29] It has often been replaced by a polite shared responsibility which extends to social kindnesses like watching the house while the neighbours are away, even though we may not actually know their names. Indeed, 'Many specifically choose *not* to "know" their spatial neighbours in any intimate sense. This allows them more time and energy to cultivate the friends they themselves select.'[30]

Of course, the original suburban colonists did not leave the close (they would no doubt say suffocating) environment of the inner cities simply to join another close-knit community. But this aspect of suburban living seems to be the result of a mixture of other ingredients too.

One is the suburban redefinition of 'neighbourhood.' A majority of suburbanites still work at a distance from where they live. An ever-increasing majority of their time is spent with people whose homes are nowhere near their own. Networks are replacing community in modern suburbia.

The loss of suburban social cohesion has been unwittingly accelerated by recent (and laudable) Government policies designed to inject funds for social inclusion and the like into areas of obvious deprivation. In this climate it is precisely the suburban areas which will have no community centres, because they are 'not seen as political priorities.'[31] According to an article in *The Times*: 'The suburbs are the black sheep of regeneration; planners and Government are far keener on filleting and cleaning our inner cities.'[32]

In addition, the widespread belief nowadays that nobody is an expert on anything has led to a breakdown of trust: 'Instead of letting children walk to school, when they might bump into their neighbours, parents will want to drive them. Trust will be extended only to those we know. Neighbours will remain strangers, kept at a distance.'[33] In the young this mistrust is particularly acute: 'The trend for deconstructing everyone and everything has left us with no heroes to follow, and so most young people are more likely to know what is no longer worth believing in than to have a positive and clear idea of what they do actually believe.'[34] Increasingly suspicious both of individuals and of institutions, people are more and more wary of any commitment. The increasing divorce rate and dwindling marriage rate both testify to this, as do the rapidly reducing numbers of volunteers in any sphere. The wariness of change which has long been recognized as a feature of suburban life[35] has been aggravated by this culture of mistrust. So better not let the neighbours in.

The flood of working women has also contributed to the loss of a sense of community in suburbia. Historically it has been women who have woven the fabric of society. Nowadays they are often struggling to maintain a household and a full-time paid job. It is a sea-change which has happened in just one generation. Frank McCourt struggles to explain it to his mother:

> She made tea in a teapot and couldn't help sniffing at the idea of teabags. I told her teabags were just a convenience for people with busy lives and she said no-one is so busy they can't take time to make a decent cup of tea for what is it all about anyway? Are we put into this world to be busy or to chat over a nice cup of tea?[36]

A psychologist writes: 'We live in a society where people are more likely to be economically successful if they can cultivate individual enterprise, independence and some ability to disregard their own feelings and other people's...Not surprisingly, in the present century loneliness and disorientation have become major psychological problems.'[37] On the whole, this fundamental sociological change has yet to hit the inner-cities, where housing is cheaper and dual-income households not yet the norm.

For Discussion

1 How well do these trends match the area served by your church?
2 Why do people come to live in your area? How long do they stay?
3 What do people value highly? How does this relate to gospel values?
4 Do you regard yourselves as suburbanites? If yes, are there ways in which you aim to differ from your neighbours? If no, what tactics could your church adopt to reach out to its neighbours?

Suburbia:
Bad News for the Church

3

The picture painted is one with which many of us are familiar, even comfortable.

It is, in short, 'normality.' And that is probably the reason why many of us find ourselves bewildered by the struggles encountered in recent years by the churches in suburbia. 'The churches in the west have never been able to attract equal numbers of people from right across the social spectrum, but today we cannot attract the very people who, sociologically and culturally, were the mainstay of the church even as recently as the middle of the twentieth century.'[38] Yet we are doing things in just the same way which always worked so well.

Perhaps the past 'success' of the suburban church is part of what we are up against now. Undoubtedly we have grown complacent in a way which is denied to those struggling to lead churches in our inner-cities. In some churches we have become flabby and unfit, expecting that there will rarely be any need to flex our Christian muscles. We soak up biblical teaching; we attend courses and Christian conferences; we hold meetings to discuss evangelism. Yet growth—in quantity or quality—stubbornly refuses to come.

Before we can make an attempt to establish any kind of strategy for the suburban church, we need to take a look at some of the factors which might be contributing to making the whole process so hard. It is admittedly a rather depressing exercise, but it may be an important step on the way to understanding the culture in which we are set.

New Value-System

'Most of our way of church life as Protestant Christians was formulated in the late Enlightenment and early modern period. This time is gone. The pace of change means that we have to play more than catch up; we have to engage in radical change.'[39] In particular, as we have seen, during the past 30 or so years the whole suburban value-system has been transformed, and the church is in danger of not noticing. Some of these changes in values have already been mentioned, but the following are among the most significant.

1 Things Matter More Than People
We live in a suburban society where many people are indifferent to the Christian values which have underpinned British culture for centuries. In a recent

interview, Cardinal Cormac Murphy O'Connor described it: 'You see quite a demoralised society, one where the only good is what I want, the only rights are my own, and the only life with any meaning or value is the life I want for myself.'[40] This succinctly describes the new ethos of suburbia. Silverstone describes how suburbia offers 'a new kind of neo-participatory politics based on self-interest and grounded in defensive anxiety.'[41] In short, a tacit atheism prevails. If we were to take this one fact properly on board, it might transform our whole way of being church there.

2 Individualism is Steadily Replacing Community

'We're too busy to have any community spirit,' ran a recent headline in our local paper. Sadly this attitude is also common in our churches. 'Individualism...manifests itself in church life when people start to believe that their own needs are of far greater importance than the Christian community to which they belong.'[42]

> Too often being a Christian means being squeaky clean, always respectable, well-dressed—and usually without much joy...The church cannot afford to have many people pretending not to need grace, and still have any sense of community.[43]

Peter Price contrasts this with the sense of belonging in churches elsewhere: 'The church among the poor has a greater commitment to community and to the sharing of possessions. The fellowship of the poor regards each as belonging to one family.'[44] It was back in 1961 that Gibson Winter wrote of churches in suburban America, but many of his observations are startlingly apposite to UK suburbs today. In particular he talks about what he calls the 'organization church,' which arises from 'the peculiar coalition between the major denominations and the emerging middle-class.' Among other features which we shall glimpse later, this style of church 'does not require intimate relationships among members to sustain its internal life.'[45]

Close community in the suburban church is in any case adversely affected by the need of its members to protect themselves from each other. Mark Stibbe compares it with Aldous Huxley's Brave New World, ' a society in which there seems to be no pain...in which reality is not allowed to surface for a moment.'[46] Authenticity is much harder to achieve in this context, so 'bearing one another's burdens' often becomes an impossibility, even for the church leaders paid to do it.

3 Idolatry is Alive and Kicking

'In their pursuit of prosperity, salvation, health, protection and so forth, people sooner or later create gods.'[47] Material possessions, striven for at a sometimes considerable cost, take on a disproportionate importance. The percentage of private homes equipped with burglar alarms in England and Wales doubled between 1992 and 2000. What we value we must protect. When the teenagers' confirmation class is held a t our house, 12 pairs of trainers are queued up in the hall while their occupants sit in their socks, protecting the precious carpet as they have been taught. There is a certain irony in the fact that the removal of shoes, in Christian and other religions, has traditionally indicated the presence of the holy. With amazing prescience, George Orwell wrote in 1936:

> Money-worship has been elevated into a religion. Perhaps it is the only real religion—the only really *felt* religion—that is left to us. Money is what God used to be. Good and evil have no meaning any longer except failure and success. Hence the profoundly significant phrase, *to make good*.[48]

Suburbia is full of people—in churches and outside them—who have *made good*. And that in its turn subtly redefines theology: 'Where money is an idol, to be poor is a sin' (William Stringfellow). It is much harder for suburban Christians than for their UPA counterparts to fight against this alien god which threatens to dethrone the Living One. That presents the church with a major headache: 'Business as usual in the church is not going to save us as long as foreign gods are set up in our sanctuaries.'[49]

4 The Need for Control

As we have seen above, this is one of suburbia's founding principles. Its inhabitants plan. It is the only way they can run their busy lives successfully. 'Even the weekend is regimented into the structures of the working week, fundamentally being undermined by the same forces that created and sustained it.'[50] And the church benefits—up to a point. In the macro, that point is reached when services and church events are planned so far ahead that there is no room for flexibility, manoeuvre or alteration. ('Is the church as we know it just too bland, dull and safely predictable for those who crave an experience of radical change?' asks Drane.[51]) On a smaller scale, it overreaches itself when it removes the possibility for any spontaneous happening during the service. In those churches aspiring to be 'charismatic' this will cause especial difficulties. What about the Holy Spirit, whose wind 'blows where it will'? A recent commentator on the NHS made the point that it is now 'all systems and structures, but no kindness.' It is sad to reflect that the same accusation could be levelled at some of our suburban churches. Peter Price observes that: 'The rich and powerful are trapped in their need to control resources, events and circumstances. The cross of Christ offers an alternative—the relinquishment of wealth and control in order to choose servanthood and humility.'[52] Whilst it is by no means a rule that suburbanites have vast wealth to relinquish, the principle still holds.

One serious casualty of the tight control we have examined tends to be a sense of fun, which has about it an inherent spontaneity. To their credit, many suburban churches realize the lack and attempt to re-establish opportunities for 'fun' planned at 6-monthly intervals into the programme. Somehow, though, it's not quite the same.

Outdated Expectations

Accompanying these undergirding principles there is in the churches a whole set of expectations which have been inherited from previous generations, but which no longer hold true. If we acknowledged this, it would help us to transform our ways of operating in suburbia. Here are some examples.

1 Self-worth
For centuries churches have been accepted as a source of identity, self-worth or friendship for their adherents. While it often still applies in UPAs, this has been turned on its head in suburbia. Its people derive their esteem from their paid jobs, their identity and friendships from the gym or the golf-club— places where admitting allegiance to a church is more likely to undermine others' esteem than enhance it. In suburbia our sense of value may be derived from our faith, but seldom any longer from belonging to the church. As for those corporate achievers in our parishes who have no faith: 'Such people paradoxically often end up with little sense of self-worth or individual identity, both of them having been sacrificed to the corporate image and the constant striving for "success."'[53]

2 Children's Work
Children and young people, once a fertile seed-bed for Christian faith, are now, as we have seen, too busy. Years back, it was a safe assumption that children would come to Sunday School (or its equivalent) because it was less boring than being at home. That just will not wash any longer in suburbia, where the alternative activities might include horse-riding, seeing an absent parent, a shopping spree or even catching up with the weekend's homework. Churches offer no accreditation for the National Record of Achievement! Even Christian parents (and this is hard to accept) have often been so overtaken by the new suburban value-system that taking their children to church on Sunday is seen as a last resort when the exciting options run out. For their older offspring a living faith can come lower down a suburban Christian parent's value-hierarchy than a good set of A-level results. All this adds up to very patchy Christian teaching for our young people.

3 Eclectic Congregations
Most churches no longer contain a cross-section of the community. The homogeneity of many suburban areas, plus the suburban culture of choice linked

with car ownership on a vast scale means that each congregation is in some way self-selecting. In true suburban style, newcomers will be attracted where they see 'people like us.' 'The congregation is first and foremost an economic peer-group; it is secondarily a believing and worshipping community.'[54] It is no longer safe, either, to assume that there will be representatives of every age-group in any suburban congregation. Generation X, almost all car-owners, are quick to take themselves to church where they find others of their age-group. These imbalances happen less readily in the inner-city, where selection still operates mostly on the level of residency.

4 Neighbourhood?

Many churches (and in particular the Church of England) still operate as though they cater for the needs of a particular neighbourhood. While this is even now the case with the occasional offices in parish churches, in the rest of suburban church life it is increasingly unrealistic. 'The street has become part of the public sphere, and therefore an area for which the individual is not responsible.'[55] A majority of suburbanites still work at a distance from where they live. An ever-increasing majority of their time is spent with people whose homes are nowhere near their own. 'Neighbourhoods of birth' comments Moynagh, 'are giving way to neighbourhoods of choice.'[56] 'Neighbourhood' has been largely neglected in favour of 'networks.' It is to these networks—the ones they themselves choose—that suburbanites are willing to give their leisure time, often disproportionately lavishly.

5 Visiting

In many cultures it is considered to be a valued compliment for someone to call at the house. Even in British suburbia that was the state of play until recently. But cold-calling at doors in some suburban areas is now totally unacceptable. It is seen as an unwelcome intrusion into residents' privacy as well as a disruption of a carefully prepared routine, and will more often damage the church than encourage new members. Sadly this applies just as much to dog-collar wearers—indeed, that may make the call even less welcome. The discomfort of the occupier will seldom be verbalized, but actions speak louder... ('Why,' asked our bemused 8-year-old after a new move to suburbia, 'don't they just tell us to eff off?'). We really need to revise our ideas about how to contact outsiders!

6 Leadership and Body Ministry

The position of ordained church leaders in suburban society has changed dramatically. Even in our last UPA parish, where the sad history of the church should have provoked severe anti-clericalism, my husband was accorded first respect and soon affection by the local (secular) neighbourhood. In our current suburban parish the most frequent first response to his dog-collar is mistrust. 'In a postmodern society,' claims Edmondson, 'trust is built on relationships, not authority and institution.'[57] If this is the case, then it combines unhealthily with the difficulty of making local relationships for which the congregation has no time. The problem is compounded, too, by the requirement on many ordained church leaders of various mainstream denominations that they move from church to church every four or five years.

In addition, within the suburban church the approach to ordained leaders is confusingly inconsistent. Philip Richter has pointed out a subtle but important distinction between first- and second-generation suburbanites, observing in particular the effect on approaches to those in positions of authority:

- The *established* middle-class: themselves the product of suburbia; confident about their place in society; ready to accept others' authority if it is well exercised or to share it if appropriate.
- The *emergent* middle-class: the product of more humble home backgrounds; '...apparently middle-class professionals...uneasy in their relationships with other professionals, and uncomfortable in the social settings of suburbia;'[58] ambivalent towards authority figures, whom they simultaneously respect and resent.

Making assumptions here can be particularly dangerous for those clergy or leaders who aim to become *enablers* of the body of Christ. Some suburban congregations will be very happy to enter into body ministry, some will warm to it in the end, but some will refuse point blank on the grounds that he or she is 'paid to do it.' Winter points out another reason for the diminishing of lay ministry: 'The more introverted the church, the more it becomes subject to priestcraft and routinized activities...The captivity of the church behind the suburban curtain transmutes the lay ministry into mere contributors to the machinery of the local organization.'[59]

7 Volunteers
The churches—especially in suburbia—have always been able to rely on a good number of volunteer lay members to share the necessary tasks. Volunteering is declining everywhere, but nowhere is the change more stark than in suburbia, where—as those who lead suburban churches will know—volunteers are thin on the ground. Because time is so short, anything resonant of duty or responsibility in one's leisure time is to be avoided. As we have seen, even the young retired, once a fertile harvest-field for volunteers, are often busy looking after their children's children for much of the week. In our current church, deputies are much easier to find than the postholders themselves. Belonging is demonstrated by being on a rota—nobody does anything (unpaid) every week. This means that those tasks which involve

the creation and sustaining of relationships (children's work, for example) are increasingly being abandoned by lay-people. Professional (that is, paid) workers are being hired in their place in much the same way—and for the same reason—as many of our neighbours subcontract their domestic cleaning.

8 Village Meets Suburb

Suburbs are sometimes created with alarming speed. Our current parish is not untypical; the transformation from village to suburb has happened in just one generation. This leaves on the one hand a shrinking population who believe (still) that they live in a village, and on the other a fast-growing population of suburbanites. The church, which has traditionally represented the village, is in danger of continuing to cater for this section of its population without regard to the other, larger one. Where change has happened so quickly, it is easy for long-time resident Christians not even to realize that the newcomers actually think and function differently from them. This is a challenge for evangelism!

For Discussion

1 How can we as individual Christians make a stand against the materialism of suburbia?
2 What might it mean for the church to have a prophetic role in suburbia?
3 What are some of the implications of being church in an atheistic society?
4 What is your attitude to your clergy and church leaders?

4

The Church:
Good News for Suburbia?

The suburban church has a problem, then.

In the interests of the gospel, St Paul became 'all things to all men' (I Cor 9: 19–23). Yet there is a serious conflict here: 'Suburbia revealed by social analysis has a different agenda from the gospel.'[60] If we follow St Paul's example (and, in many cases, our own upbringing) we are in danger of endorsing a set of values which are in direct conflict with the gospel of Christ. But if, on the other hand, we distance ourselves too much from the culture around us we shall seem cranky and irrelevant.

Respectaburbia

As we have seen, the church no longer has the respect or authority among the general population of suburbia to exercise its traditional prophetic role. 'Western societies have become far more resistant to the gospel than the pre-Christian paganism with which cross-cultural missions have been familiar.'[61] The suburban desire for *respectability* once found an expression in churchgoing, giving suburban churches at least a perceived advantage over their inner-city counterparts. Nowadays, when churchgoing is no longer an embodiment of suburban respectability, what remains is the down side of 'respectaburbia': 'It is much easier to repent if one is obviously bad; virtue conceals the freedom of God—one might think one had deserved his grace. It is, therefore a disadvantage to be respectable.'[62] 'Whatever God wants in our relationship with him,' asserts H A Williams, 'it certainly isn't respectability.'[63]

Scratching Where People Itch

And yet all around us in suburbia is evidence of a yearning for God. 'Spirituality' is the in-word in schools and secular youth leadership circles. Our local FE college capitalizes on the burgeoning interest in 'alternative spiritualities' by offering classes in Tai Chi, Indian Head Massage, Reiki, Astrology, Crystal healing, Aromatherapy...and the list is expanding. Recent research done by interviewing random members of the public in Nottingham has revealed an unexpected escalation in spiritual awareness:

Frequency of Report of Religious or Spiritual Experience in Britain for the Years 1987 and 2000[64]		
	1987	2000
A patterning of events	29%	55%
Awareness of the presence of God	27%	38%
Awareness of prayer being answered	25%	37%
Awareness of a sacred presence in nature	16%	29%
Awareness of the presence of the dead	18%	25%
Awareness of an evil presence	12%	25%

Perhaps there is some accuracy in George Herbert's imagined words from God on materialism:

> Yet let him keep the rest,
> But keep them with repining restlessness:
> Let him be rich and weary, that at least
> If goodness lead him not, yet weariness
> May toss him to my breast.[65]

It is dangerous to fall into the trap of assuming that falling church attendances mean spiritual apathy. 'While it is not the case that suburbia is profoundly religious, the inherent discontent and longing for the new makes people open to the possibilities of a spiritual journey...Here lies the field "white unto harvest."'[66] The challenge for the suburban church is to find a way of scratching where people itch.

How, then, do we become truly incarnational[67] in 21st-century suburbia as Jesus himself did in 1st-century Palestine? Suppose there was a way for the church to bring God back into the suburban spiritual vacuum without selling its soul.

Each time an Alpha course runs in our suburban parish, a handful of new Christians emerge. But these same Alpha graduates (unlike those in our inner-city experience) rarely become regular church attenders. 'The group wants to stay together,' we have argued, so over the years we have devised more and more programmes (Beta, Gamma,...) for the group to do midweek. So we create yet another separate congregation. Why are these new Alpha-bred Christians so church-resistant?

Church—Work or Play?

Michael Moynagh observes that people in 21st-century Britain tend to vacillate between two different mindsets, partly depending on their context at any given time.[68] I have adapted these below. *Work* (and education) *Mode*, involves expectations totally different from its counterpart, *Leisure Mode*. It is important to note that neither mode operates to the exclusion of the other and neither is inherently good or bad. Suburbanites face more of a tension between the two, being more skilled than their WYSIWYG ('what you see is what you get') city counterparts in adopting a different persona according to context.

Work Mode	Leisure Mode
Aim: efficiency	Aim: enjoyment
Doing	Being
Control	Spontaneity
Competitiveness/defensiveness	Friendship/openness
Achievement (targets)	People values
Serious professionalism	Fun
Obligation/duty	Choice
Objective facts important	Feelings important
Word-dominated	Image-dominated
Meetings	Meals/celebrations
Stress	Relaxation
Utilitarian	Dilettante

The previous chapters have outlined a number of characteristics of suburbia which are unhelpful to the life of the church there. It is interesting to observe how many of them feature in the left-hand list. *Work mode* is very important to suburbanites because:

- where a high percentage of the population is in (or has retired from) employment or education, workplace values are never far away.
- the Protestant Ethic, filtered from one generation to another, is high on the agenda for many suburban dwellers.

But most suburbanites have learned to counterbalance this by spending lavishly on their leisure. Stress-reducing hobbies such as gardening, exercising and travel are on the increase, a recent Mintel British Lifestyles Survey observed.[69] Suburbia's cash-rich, time-poor residents often take four or five holidays in a year. They spend vast annual subscriptions to belong to health clubs where they can 'chill out' before or after a long day at the office. They do not begrudge the expenditure of time or of money in order to flip for a few precious hours from *work mode* to *leisure mode*. They work hard and they play hard. 'Liberation from the bonds of the present system takes place by playing games.'[70] Enjoyment, too, is important to suburbanites.

Church as Work

Where in the dichotomy does the suburban church fit? Look at the two lists again, this time bearing in mind the ways in which your church operates:

* How are church 'meetings' conducted?
* What clothes do members of the congregation wear?
* Are training courses more regular than social gatherings?

The chances are that your church functions for most of the time in *work mode*, especially if it belongs to one of the older denominations. 'The search for meaning through activity and performance is typically middle-class...To be a middle-class Christian is to perform well on the committee.'[71]

In other words, what we are offering our congregations in their free time is more of what makes up the rest of their week—committee meetings, paperwork, obligation and stress. The reason, it is said, why there are not more people going into church may well be the look on the faces of those coming out. The suburban church is in danger of matching Gibson Winter's sad caricature: 'a treadmill where men and women grind out their salvation.'[72] This is impressed on a suburban church leader every time he or she approaches a reluctant layperson to become PCC secretary or churchwarden; every time a member of the congregation asks to 'come off the rota' for this or that job; every school holiday when large numbers of the congregation need to take 'time off' church; every time the golf club proves to be a greater draw than the weekly Bible study.

We are offering our congregation in their free time more of what makes up the rest of their week

Church as Play

By way of contrast, glance across at any suburban church you know which seems to function more meaningfully. Is it perhaps because people actually enjoy being part of it? One of the reasons for Alpha's huge success has been its emphasis on friendship, eating together and fun. If people enjoy coming to Alpha (in *leisure mode*), is it any surprise that they react when we expect them suddenly to change to *work mode* by going to Sunday services?

Are Fun and Christian Discipleship Compatible?

Anyone who been touched by God has experienced a profound passion and joy, however momentary. The lifestyle of Jesus recorded in the gospels hints that he was not anti-fun. In fact, rather the reverse seems to have been true—

meals, parties, barbecues on the beach, gatherings with friends. In his high-priestly prayer, Jesus asks his Father 'that [his followers] might have the full measure of my joy within them' (Jn 17:13). Yet many Christians have acquired a reputation for having a joy so deep that it is unfathomable. Why else would the title of Edward Schillebeeckx's book, 'I am a Happy Theologian,' be so striking?

Why else would 'I a a Happy Theologian be so striking?

'Unless you change and become like little children,' Jesus said, 'you will never enter the kingdom of heaven' (Mt 18:3). One of the marks of a child is surely the innocent ability to play and have fun without guilt. The same unfettered playfulness is found amongst those with learning difficulties, too. The suburban church could do worse than take time to learn from these 'Clowns of God.'[73] When David danced before God, it is unlikely to have been out of a sense of duty. 'The glorification of God lies in the demonstrative joy of existence,' claims Moltmann.[74] In Tomlin's words: 'Miserable, dull and gloomy churches have simply missed the point.'[75]

Clearly I am not advocating an irresponsible and reckless hedonism. 'True celebration is the inverse of hedonism,' points out John Ortberg, explaining that hedonism causes our capacity for joy to diminish, while celebration increases our ability to enjoy the simplest gifts of God.[76] If joy and fun are a natural expression of our response to God, then the churches do God's people a major disservice if they teach the opposite. 'Joylessness...may be the sin most readily tolerated by the church,' says Ortberg.'[77]

To encourage a sense of joy is not to deny the pain in the world— quite the reverse is true

To encourage a sense of joy, even of fun, is not to deny the pain in the world—and in our churches and communities. Quite the reverse is true. One reason why lithium carbonate has become such a useful drug for the treatment of manic-depression is that it suppresses both the highs and lows of the emotional spectrum. But the resultant impassivity is mirrored dangerously by some expressions of routine suburban Christianity. 'Only those who are capable of joy can feel pain at their own and other people's suffering.'[78] It has many times been pointed out that, for all their tragic and suffering history, the Jewish nation understands the true nature of celebration better than many. This is precisely why Karl Barth describes joy as 'a defiant nevertheless.' A Sunday service we shared in an Anglo-Catholic church in the Johannesburg township of Sebokeng last year simply bounced with irrepressible joy. 'Joy and love are...of the essence of creation...sin and suffering are invasive and parasitical.'[79]

Changing the Mindset

Suppose your church could move its emphasis from *work mode* to *leisure mode*. What would that mean in practice? Some examples:

- A Vineyard church outside Leeds meets monthly at 11am at the local David Lloyd health club. It advertises (on beer mats): 'bouncy castle, cappuccino, worship, shared lunch, ministry, teaching, football, swim and gym.'

- An Anglican church in suburban Shrewsbury has an unusual approach to its AGM. Held on a Sunday, it starts with a service and coffee, moving onto the bare minimum of essential business while the children are entertained with games. A communal lunch follows, then a kind of church expo, where each ministry has a stand, using a variety of demonstrations and presentations to show creatively what they do and how, and taking names of anyone interested in joining the team. It is described as 'exciting' and 'great fun!'

- Every so often one of the new churches in a town in Derbyshire puts on a pantomime in a local venue on a Sunday evening. A gifted member of the congregation writes the script, which includes a number of Christian songs, some specially written. Tickets are sold locally for £1 each. On arrival everyone is given a 'Celebration' chocolate, and at the interval drinks and bags of sweets are distributed. The sense of fun is infectious and the Christian message is inescapable.

These approaches might seem radical, but they demonstrate that it is not impossible to change a congregation's (or indeed a community's) mindset in their approach to church. They all bear the hallmark of celebration, a shared joy in God.

Yes, But How?

Clearly this is not a change which can be accomplished overnight in any church, and contexts vary. Yet there are pointers which might help make the transition in any context:

Food and Drink: If people are eating and/or drinking with friends, they are very soon in *leisure mode* in spite of themselves. It works for Alpha! Suppose a Sunday gathering were to be set out with chairs around coffee tables instead of in serried ranks of chairs/pews. Why not start with coffee and a-little-something instead of adding it on afterwards when the congregation is keen to rush off to get lunch? What about a break in the middle? There is nothing inherently unworshipful about this—Jesus spent many happy hours with his disciples eating and drinking while he talked them through the gospel.

Involvement not Spectating: 'God made man because he loves stories,' comments the novelist Elie Wiesel. Our suburban congregation comes closest to 'koinonia'—community—when an individual tells his or her story during the service. But what was a common occurrence in our UPA parishes is treated as a huge risk in suburbia, and it seems that the only way to break down this particular barrier is to keep making space for it in worship until the congregation begins to feel comfortable with it and appreciate its benefits. 'In the kind of pluralistic world inhabited by the first Christians, it was stories and community that made the difference.'[80]

Attitude of Church Leaders: It would be neither true nor fair to suggest that the personality of the leader of a church determined the mindset of its congregation. But many of our church leaders have themselves been conditioned by successive suburban congregations into losing their innate sense of fun—an attribute rarely missing among theological college students! Perhaps some could give themselves permission to unearth it *for the benefit of the gospel...*

Creativity: Our Father delights in it. Do we in our churches? Or is it simply another burdensome activity for which there is no time? Why are so many of our churches (especially the evangelical ones) such a damaging mixture of utilitarianism and Puritanism that we are no longer able to glory in beauty if it is seen as unnecessary? This is work mode at its most unhealthy. Suburbia needs creativity because 'The creative play of expression does not depend on successes and accomplishments.'[81]

Time: The timetables of our churches can be terrifying. In activist suburbia we get sucked into work mode in this regard more than any other. The congregation knows its duty, and its duty is to meet as many church 'appointments' as possible in the week. On Sunday, the expectation of the leaders seems to imply, it is the duty of all 'committed' members of the congregation to be present at every service. And indeed this was the expectation of many a churchgoer a generation ago. Nowadays suburban life is too full for that, for a variety of reasons which do not all relate to lack of Christian commitment. If only churches could stop putting unrealistic guilt-trips on their members and instead drastically reduce the number of meetings and services each week, Christians might truly begin to enjoy 'times of calm, quiet and stillness to create a space where they can wait on God and recentre their fragmented and conflicted lives.'[82]

Possible Consequences

If it were possible then, over time, to reorient a church's communal dominant mindset from *work mode* to *leisure mode*, its lifestyle might mirror more faithfully the God we worship. But what about other by-products of the change?

Inside...

The most dramatic would undoubtedly be that the congregation could start to enjoy coming to church. And people make time for what they find enjoyable. This alone has mind-blowing implications in a church where, outside their paid jobs, lay people have very little time to give to anything else which could be labelled 'duty.' What little spare time they have is not unreasonably allocated to enjoyment and relaxation. If being an active part of God's family in Xburb were fun, then we might even find that our **lay-staffing problems** went some way towards being solved. 'The difficulty felt by many people...is not so much about the amount of time that might be involved, as the quality of the experience in relation to the time they have invested.'[83]

There might be other knock-on effects. If parents are obviously enjoying themselves, children very often find themselves caught up in the same spirit. There is a huge chasm between the church where children are reluctantly dragged until they are old enough to refuse, and the (much rarer) churches I have occasionally attended where **children clearly enjoy being there** as much as their parents.

Once people start to function in leisure mode, they automatically begin to drop their guard. We are all capable of putting on masks when we are on our best behaviour, and in suburbia we are on our best behaviour more often than elsewhere. But people who are relaxed will be themselves. Gradually they will feel the **freedom to be vulnerable**. And reality will be reflected when they get together, whatever form that takes.

The need for **community** for both physical and psychological health is one which has been proved over many years.[84] Until recently that need was answered by churches. Nowadays suburban churches might learn a profitable lesson from the many UPAs where it still is: '[in] the simplicity of neighbourhoods [that] Christian people witness, worship, pray and speak into their own situation. The problem of individualism which confronts us does not confront them...Learning solidarity demands unlearning our individualism.'[85] Many of us have observed the difference that comes over a congregation which has been away together for a church houseparty, Spring Harvest, Grapevine or Cursillo—having fun together in Christ. Imagine that same sense of togetherness being generated at every church function! Christians in our congregations might even start to enjoy each other's company to the extent that they start to rediscover the lost art of **hospitality**, because they will realize that offering a meal is a gift of love and not an examination to be passed. It is all about love, and no longer competition or defensiveness:

> Loving others is not possible unless I am myself loved. Only then will I feel a secure sense of worth, of being valued, so that I can go out and relate to others without needing them to confirm my sense of worth.[86]

In short, Jesus' words about his giving rest to those who are stressed might really be lived out in his church.

...And Outside

This may be beginning to sound too cosy and introspective to be a real reflection of the body of Christ. But it is only the beginning of the story.

The *real* benefits of a shift into leisure mode are its knock-on effects on secular suburbia. Suddenly the saltiness might be restored to the salt of the earth. Imagine what would result if people outside the church could see that Christians...

- enjoyed their lives and were excited by their churches.
- were no longer embarrassed to invite others to learn more about the source of all this joy.
- were genuinely among the least stressed people around.
- had found a deep spirituality which worked.

For Discussion:

1 Do you agree that God is pro-fun? Why or why not?
2 Compare the two lists in this chapter. Where do the hallmarks of your church fit?
3 Would it help to change the ethos of your church gatherings?
4 What practical steps might this involve?
5 What might be the practical effects of adopting leisure mode in your church's context?

Let the Son of God grow in you.
Let Him become in you a smile
And laughter
And perfect joy
That no-one can take from you.[87]

Notes

1   Tony Parsons, *Man and Boy* (Harper Collins, London, 2000) p 32.
2   Michael Gwilliam, 'Sustainable Suburbs, Joseph Rowntree Foundation Report' in *Findings* (JRF, February 1999).
3   See Benson and Roberts, Grove Pastoral booklet P 92 *Counting Sheep*.
4   Andrew Marr, 'Life on the Edge' (article in *The Observer* 9 January 2000).
5   Walmsley and Lewis, *Human Geography—Behavioural Approaches* (Longman, 1984).
6   Roger Silverstone, *Visions of Suburbia* (Routledge, London, 1997) p 4.
7   Michael Moynagh and Richard Worsley, *Tomorrow* (Lexicon, Kings Lynn, 2000) pp 23, 28.
8   See note 2.
9   Figures from the 1991 UK Census of Population.
10 Gibson Winter, *The Suburban Captivity of the Churches* (Doubleday, New York) p 65.
11 Robert Fishman, *Bourgeois Utopia—a history of the suburb* (Basic Books, 1989).
12 Moynagh and Worsley, *Tomorrow* p 80.
13 J A Walter, *A Long Way from Home* (Paternoster, Exeter 1979) p 82.
14 T S Eliot, *Four Quartets*.
15 Mark Stibbe, *O Brave New Church* (DLT, London, 1995) p 16.
16 Philip Richter, *God's Here and Now* (DLT, London, 1999) p 84.
17 J A Walter, *A Long Way from Home* p 70.
18 Andre Godin, *The Psychological Dynamics of Religious Experience* (Religious Education Press, Alabama, 1985) p 26.
19 Moynagh and Worsley, *Tomorrow* p 85.
20 Gibson Winter, *The Suburban Captivity* p 75.
21 'Sun, Sangria and my Psion' in *The Times*, 24 July 2001.
22 Roger Silverstone, *Visions of Suburbia* p 8.
23 Roger Silverstone, *Visions of Suburbia* p 52.
24 Michael Moynagh, *Changing World, Changing Church* (Monarch, London, 2001) p 76.
25 John Drane, *The McDonaldisation of the Church* (DLT, London 2000) p 24.
26 Richard Keyes, *Chameleon or Tribe?* (IVP, Leicester, 1999) p 119.
27 Philip Richter, *God's Here and Now* pp 81–2.
28 Lipman and Russell-Lacy 1974, quoted in Walmsley and Lewis, *Human Geography*.
29 Gibson Winter, *The Suburban Captivity* p 88.
30 Harvey Cox in M Northcott (ed), *Urban Theology: A Reader* (Cassell, London, 1998) p 68.
31 See note 2.
32 Tim Teeman, *The Times*, August 28 1999.
33 Moynagh and Worsley, *Tomorrow* p 87.
34 John Drane, *The McDonaldisation of the Church* p 64.
35 See note 2.
36 Frank McCourt, *'Tis* (Flamingo, London 1999) p 388.
37 J Klein, *Our Need for Others and its Roots in Infancy* (Routledge, London, 1987) p 100–101.
38 John Drane, *The McDonaldisation of the Church* p 12.
39 James Thwaites, *The Church Beyond the Congregation* (Paternoster, Carlisle, 1999) p 25.

40 Interview in *The Times*, 6 September 2001.
41 Roger Silverstone, *Visions of Suburbia* p 12.
42 Mark Stibbe, *O Brave New Church* p 95.
43 Richard Keyes, *Chameleon or Tribe?* (IVP Leicester, 1999) p 111.
44 Peter Price, *The Church as Kingdom* (Zondervan/Marshall Pickering, 1987) p 33.
45 Gibson Winter, *The Suburban Captivity* p 92.
46 Mark Stibbe, *O Brave New Church* p 16.
47 Goudzwaard, *Idols of Our Time* (IVCF, Illinois, 1984) p 13.
48 George Orwell, *Keep the Aspidistras Flying* (1936) p 46.
49 Howard Snyder in his foreword to Goudzwaard, *Idols of Our Time* p 8.
50 Roger Silverstone, *Visions of Suburbia* p 18.
51 John Drane, *The McDonaldisation of the Church* p 28.
52 Peter Price, *The Church as Kingdom* p 130.
53 John Drane, *The McDonaldisation of the Church* p 73.
54 Gibson Winter, *The Suburban Captivity* p 71.
55 J A Walter, *A Long Way from Home* p 55.
56 Moynagh and Worsley, *Tomorrow* p 86.
57 Chris Edmondson, Grove Pastoral booklet P 83 *Minister, Love Thyself* p 3.
58 Philip Richter, *God's Here and Now* p 81.
59 Gibson Winter, *The Suburban Captivity* pp 104, 152.
60 Philip Richter, *God's Here and Now* p 97.
61 Newbiggin, *Foolishness to the Greeks* (1986).
62 Fenton, *The Matthew Passion* (BRF, Oxford, 1995) p 46.
63 H A Williams, *Tensions* (Mitchell Beazley, London, 1979) p 31.
64 David Hay and Kate Hunt, *Adult Spirituality Project* (University of Nottingham, 2000).
65 George Herbert, *The Pulley*.
66 Philip Richter, *God's Here and Now* p 82.
67 Defined as 'expressing what God's rule means in a particular local setting' by Tomlin, *The Provocative Church* (SPCK, London, 2002) p 82.
68 Michael Moynagh, *Changing World* p 49ff.
69 Report in *The Times* 29 January 2003.
70 Jürgen Moltmann, *Theology and Joy* (SCM, London, 1973) p 36.
71 Gibson Winter, *The Suburban Captivity* p 101.
72 *Ibid,* p 102.
73 Title of a novel on the subject by Morris West.
74 Moltmann, *Theology and Joy* p 44.
75 Tomlin, *The Provocative Church* p 31.
76 John Ortberg, *The Life You've Always Wanted* (Zondervan, Michigan, 2002) p 67.
77 *Ibid* p 64.
78 Moltmann, *Theology and Joy* p 52.
79 Brother Ramon, *Fulness of Joy* (Marshall Pickering, Basingstoke, 1988) p 6.
80 John Drane, *The McDonaldisation of the Church* p 140.
81 Moltmann, *Theology and Joy* p 45.
82 Gibbs and Coffey, *Church Next* (IVP, Leicester, 2001) p 179.
83 John Drane, *The McDonaldisation of the Church* p 42.
84 Lasker, Wolf and Potvin, *The Roseto Study* (Pennsylvania, 1992).
85 Peter Price, *The Church as Kingdom* p 156.
86 J A Walter, *A Long Way from Home* p 101.
87 Isaac of Stella.